Walking Through the Horizon

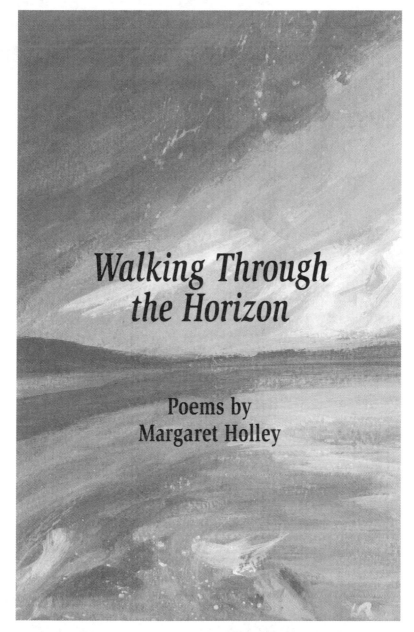

Walking Through the Horizon

Poems by
Margaret Holley

THE UNIVERSITY OF ARKANSAS PRESS • FAYETTEVILLE • 2006

Library of Congress Cataloging-in-Publication Data

Holley, Margaret.
    Walking through the horizon : poems / by Margaret Holley.
        p. cm. — (Arkansas poetry award series)
    ISBN 1-55728-812-7 (alk. paper)
    I. Title. II. Series.

PS3558.O34964W35 2006
811'.54—dc22

2005031433

For Sondra and Denise

Acknowledgments

Grateful acknowledgment is made to the editors of the following journals in which these poems first appeared, sometimes in earlier versions.

"Between Lives," "Faustian Hour," "For Sale" (published as "Moving Out"); and "Moonbath: A Lullaby," *Atlanta Review;* "The Way Home," *The Arizona Republic;* "Lattice," "Soft Touch," *Bellingham Review;* "Heart's Mountains," "Lamplight," and "Picturing Love," *Connecticut Review;* "Night Air," *The Cortland Review;* "Night Blooming in Paul Klee" (early version), *Global City Review;* "Breakfast with Bonnard," "Furnace," and "Sleeping in the Inland Sea," *Green Mountains Review;* "Angel's Landing" (Winner of the 2003 Sweet Corn Poetry Prize), *Flyway;* "Night Blooming in Paul Klee" (revised version), *Icarus International;* "Marking Time," "Phoenix," and "Reading Chopin," *The Ledge;* "Peonies," *notcoffeehouse.com;* "Frame," "The Elms of 1949," "Thank You, Edmund Waller," and "Magic," *Poem;* "Buddy," "Sleeping with Nietzsche," *Prairie Schooner;* "Walking Through the Horizon" (revised version), *Rattle;* "Eagles in Chester County," "Walking Through the Horizon" (early version), *Schuylkill Valley Journal;* "Bright Angel Point," *Southern Poetry Review;* "Hopper's *Morning Sun*," "Rereading *Four Quartets*," *The Southern Review.*

"Gibbous Moon" and "Living Water," along with several poems listed above, appeared in a chapbook, also titled *Walking Through the Horizon*, which won the 1999 Nova House Press Poetry Chapbook Award.

Contents

I. *Between Lives*

II. *The Way Home*

Walking Through the Horizon

I.

Between Lives

Sleeping with Nietzsche

In Sils Maria the water sings all night,
as it slides over stones
in iron-cold Alpine streams rippling
down the mountain toward stillness:
the lake is a tarnished mirror,
a hole in the earth full to the brim with sky.

Filling the tub with hot water, I lower myself in
beside the folded towel and terrycloth robe,
sink my head under,
and only come up for breath.
The postbus honks,
and laughter erupts downstairs in the Edelweiss.

Later, resting my head in a mountain of pillows,
I let the stream pour through it.
With a pile of books by the bed, I lie awake,
high on philosophy, high on the poetry
Nietzsche penned in this village,
high on his hopes

for the future. He is the wrong
kind of man, I think.
He'll go mad, he'll be taken up by the Nazis.
All my ghosts hang around
not knowing what to make of this liaison.
How dangerous ideas are!

Humans might not always be exactly
the kind of beings they are now.
You, starchild, will not always be
just what you are tonight.
The house sleeps with all its windows open,
and the fire that whispered

while I ate soup and bread whispers all night.
Church bells clang out the hours.
I keep the heat from the clawfoot tub
under the mound of quilt.
The mind, too, sleeps with its windows open
in the huge hotel of night,

where I incubate in the cold Alpine air
and the music of rivers all over earth,
where even the boulders dream
in their hillside,
larch needles go on turning to gold,
and the hemlocks lift and lift their heavy wings.

Breakfast with Bonnard

Blue of the 5 a.m. kitchen window
before I snap on the light, blue of the match
and the gas flame and the garden air of your *Salle
à manger sur le jardin*, antiphonal twilights,
my egg yolk and buttery toast rhyming

with your pears and croissants, your red
poppies with my jewels of strawberry jam:
your breakfast room in miniature
here in mine, where I read with my mouth full,
wiping my fingers before turning the page.

Seventy years apart, what have my
dawn and scents of coffee to do with your
1935? With the moment when Marthe
enters carrying the poppies, creating her table
just so? All these years she has been

busy at it, the garden beyond her insistently
green, sun still gilding the patch of wall,
the pears fresh in their bowl. I switch off
the radio news and turn back to you,
Pierre, as you paint dozens of these dining

room scenes, variations on a theme
of windows, tablecloths, bowls, each thing
enclosing the smaller one, nesting boxes,
your future now contained in our past,
your morning safe on the page here in mine,

and mine already there in your stained-glass
blues, your edible golds, both of us
perpetually hungry, you turning Mallarmé's
poetry into paint and me translating it back:
Home. Morning. Hope framed in a simple square.

Peonies

Where muck and worms and rampant weeds
have offered up these pink-white flowers
to a cut-glass vase, where their fragrant bed

and yours have slept side by side through more
seasons than you've ever found names for,
slept and wakened—you have grown attached

to this piece of ground. Where the red stalks
have shot up past periwinkles, hauling their recipe
for big-headed, overstuffed, swan-feathered elegance

into this meadow you've learned to call home,
here you are, about to leave, and not ready to.
Where the peonies' pale ruffles first opened

their boudoirs in the back rooms of your brain
and lit their moony globes in your sleeping forest,
you are having to be instructed yet again

in attachment: how the river clings to its banks,
how wings hold onto the rushing air, how
these blooms at the height of their glory say

Watch this! and bow their enormous heads
all the way down. Does this sound like dying?
Don't believe it. *Practice departure*, they say,

and you are already packing, blinking away rain,
mist, a blur of complacency, thinking your last
hopes have all finally wilted and crashed.

Remember how snow disappeared? Here it is,
a whole vaseful unfurling its cumulus, cupping
your face in its cool flesh and sweet winter breath.

Walking Through the Horizon

It became my definition of summer: that July
full of dog days, between jobs, between loves,
a peace of idleness and heat punctuated by lightning,
when I wandered my two rooms barefoot on wood floors,
tall windows curtained in leaves, the cricket-pulsing air
conditioned by iced drinks and the fan's hum.

Sirius the Dog Star hid all day in the lion's mane
of the sun, and with every step I took, a horizon
I had once looked forward to passed through my cells,
a subliminal verge. Sunset after sunset flew by me
unnoticed and only showed up in the west. The best
time to go out was eight or nine at night, to drive

under Montgomery Avenue's lamplit foliage, windows
down, radio low, a rising rattle of locusts escorting me
home to another long novel, its endless sentences making
my loneliness feel almost nineteenth-century, almost
someone else's. I had nothing to do but wait for fall
to haul me up to speed and tear my rapt attention

away from the nothing, the lull that it rested on,
tropical days in the doldrums, barely adrift into evening
or a tomorrow or an August that promised never
to arrive, enchanted insomniac nights of dozing
and waking in a film of sweat in a sleeping house, safe
inside its moat of ferns from any news of the world.

It's a memory I've hoarded for twenty-some years
and still claim in moments of déjà vu when time stops,
its seed case cracks open, as a storm cracks open,
a whole summer happens in one hour, and I know again
what Plato's paradise of souls awaiting rebirth is made of:
birdsong, thunder, green, cicadas, and heat.

Faustian Hour

If you knew
the number of days left to you,
would they seem any more precious than these
last days of summer, when sunlight sifts through
the oaks to splash their ghostly leaves onto the walls,
when crickets keep playing their soft sleighbell song,
and you arrive at this late Friday afternoon
with enough time
on your hands for once to make your Faustian
wish that it never end? Your husband asleep on the couch,
his mother reading her book aloud to herself in her room,
cathedrals of light enclose all of you in a pause
as long as your nearly held breath.
If you knew
you had another fifty years,
or a mere two weeks, or less, would you fill them
with counting down, these hours that are now filled
with unknown future and blessed light? Would
you, as leaves dance on the wall, and Mother's voice
drones on, and Pete lies completely still,
could you
fill that rapidly shortening time
with any more awareness, any more prayers
than now enwreathe their sleep? Light without noon's
brilliance, crickets without July's heat, dusk
without any urgency to the heaps of paper—
no, I think,
surely there can be no

more gracious hour for letting endings simply
be forgotten, as oven aromas of tarragon
and lamb arrive in the brain, that orchestral organ
now fully steeped in the pink and copper light
of a day that is going to burn immensely and forever.

Hopper's *Morning Sun*

is an uncluttered idyll, subtraction of stuff,
distilled elements: Woman. Bed. Window. Light.

Life as stillness and angles, hues and shapes.
In her sunrise pink shift, she sits hugging her knees,

while her shadow reclines in the smooth bed. Some
twentieth-century urban pastoral fantasy, I think,

slamming the book shut (then opening it again).
What dawns on us each day is my mother-in-law's

rising spiral of dementia and panic, as she sinks
into the lethe of three minutes ago, then surfaces

in the 1920s, in a two-story house in Baltimore
whose stairs are missing here in our home. She talks

to herself, telling herself long stories at my study door,
where I'm hopelessly stalled in a litter of drafts,

lurching between exasperated snap and remorse.
She refers to her son as "they," and Pete is tired of it

and angry. "This madness is ruining my life,"
he whispers to the floor. In the daily melée among us,

it's hard to tell who's more lost. Or even what it is
we're losing. The belly laugh. The art of the sequitur.

Quietly the woman in *Morning Sun* leans into the light,
riding her raft of simplicity into the day's wind.

She gazes steadily out the window, doing just
what the soul does in such hours, greeting something

both seen and unseen whose alchemies touch
everything, something serene and warm and clean.

Gibbous Moon

More than half and less than full,
the *gibbus* is the Latin *hump*,
an emblem of the odd, irregular,
my life right now, a lumpish phase,
when I can't tell whether it's waxing or waning,

the way sometimes I can't tell
whether I'm lonely or afraid or both,
and probably tired to boot, the way sometimes at 3 a.m.
I dread an early death and want the day to begin
without delay so I can forget again.

The full moon is the famous one,
but it's only a moment, like 11:18 p.m.,
a midpoint in weeks of coming and going,
leaving a less-than-perfect circle to shine on most
nights, presiding over our dreams.

I think I may not want to know
whether I'm gaining or failing. Gaining what?
Am I lonely because I'm scared? Which comes first?
Even Isaac Newton said that trying to understand
the moon's motion made his head ache.

My head says it's either humpbacked
or pregnant-bellied, not both, but the rest of me
is just grateful to glimpse at 3 a.m.
this midnight sun returning without reason,
little beauty, little returning yes.

For Sale

Three tall windows of oak, maple, and ash light.
Air astonished at emptiness, feeling around

for the usual forms, finds only open-minded space,
wall-to-wall leeway, leaf-shadowed radiance falling

on carpet freshly combed with vacuum paths.
Blond wood bookshelves wearing their lemon wax

and nothing else, their tonnage gone, echo with voices
I know by heart. Spinoza: *There is no hope without fear*

nor fear without hope. Bare walls offer themselves
to the watercolors of eastern and western skies. *Empty*

and you will be filled. Wear out and be renewed. Lao Tsu.
Each clinging philodendron tendril has been carefully

detached, each dust cloth folded full of gray fur.
Complete erasure of all traces! I'm almost incorporeal

by now—all my closely pencilled, yellowing pages
hauled away. Only memories remain to abbreviate it all,

and they depart with me at the click of the front door
lock, leaving the plea staked in the front lawn.

Between Lives

Flying westward, Philly to Phoenix,
PHL to PHX, ticker symbols for the old

and the new life, I turn my watch back
to do three hours of morning over again,

at cruising altitude on a one-way ticket,
the phase of moving where I just sit still.

I'm sure I've brought plenty of baggage,
but I've left all my keys behind, keys

that locked me in as often as they let me in.
Thus my consent to this flight. I recall

my in-laws' myna bird who would not
leave his cage. "Stand back! I'm an eagle!"

he squawked but clung to his perch.
I think of Leonardo dreaming of wings

fashioned of silk, rods, and cables,
the immense, slow-motion labor to lift one

human body into the high caravans of sky.
I wonder how much of me is still aloft

in the air of my old office, my home.
How much of me roams those rooms

at night watching leaves cover and uncover
the street lamp, watching the snow fall?

And what remnant of me is left to sit here
in this airplane 37,000 feet off the earth?

A ghost of my late self. The plane is a *bardo*,
a Buddhist place between lives, where souls

congregate, dazed, quiescent, waiting out
our forty days to rebirth—a dim metal tube

flying above the clouds with the shades down,
so many sleepers hardly suspecting the openings

toward which we travel. I'm still in love with
my past life: pin oak and red maple woods,

Pennsylvania rain percolating down into roots,
the cobbled streets of southern Switzerland,

Michigan Dutch elms sifting sunlight, birds
swooping, memory moving through what it

loves, which is all of it, hopes, grief, fear,
each narrow bed, each mansion of stars.

Strange to see us seat-belted into rows,
dozing off and on to the engines' drone,

sipping drinks, reading the world's news,
or novels, or taking in the in-flight movie,

as we leave the miles and years behind us,
like the contrail I imagine tailing this plane,

a cloud wake of leaves, crumbs, lists,
drafts flying like calendar pages, leaving too

my last qualms, the final droplets of doubt,
my myna brain with its habitual anxieties, all

evaporating over Missouri, Oklahoma,
New Mexico into the luminous blue.

Water of Life

i. Frame

My sister and I wear boys' bathing suits,
our bare chests browning in the Florida sun.

Mother wears her two-piece with the straps
tucked in. Every day we follow her slowly

half a mile up Coquina Beach and back,
picking up shells—conchs and whelks curled

tight in their houses, sand dollars drifting,
guarding their doves. A few are whole, many

are broken. I wash each one in the hissing
hem of a wave and add it to my metal pail.

The Gulf is vast. It stretches out to the horizon,
where it meets the sky, which is vaster. I

don't yet think of sky as touching us everywhere,
only as far away, at that line. After swimming

we peel off our trunks, rub down with a towel,
powder, and pull on dry suits, or sometimes

underpants. We eat our sandwiches together
on the blanket, its corners anchored by our shoes

and the beach bag. I like to arrange my shells
all around the edges of my towel—augurs

and lettered olives end to end. Then I lie
down inside their perimeter and sleep.

ii. The Elms of 1949

Two giants hold our second story in their green
shade, tinting the air of the front bedroom.

After rain, they go on raining a little, and we know
we are breathing their breath. They watch everything:

the blinking red light of the ambulance splashing
over the yard, my mother's face as she is carried

past me, strapped and blanketed on the stretcher,
angled down the stairs, loaded in, and the door shut.

They are at least a hundred years old, and I am five.
Here at my window sill, we can still feel the thud

of her bones against the floor. We hear how the air
opens its mouth wide, as the siren begins to wail.

Then the elms enfold me in their quiet world,
where eggs are cradled in nests woven of twigs,

grasses, and threads from the laundry line.
In the long silence, their leafy arms lift and settle,

weaving a spell: *You are very sleepy*, they whisper,
and we are very beautiful. When you wake, one day,

you will remember every detail of this hour. And for
the rest of your life, you will learn its endless lessons.

iii. Water of Life

Alexander the Great conquered the world
and captured a small bottle of the water of life

that could cure the king and bring the dead back
to life. Over time, the tale goes, he forgot

about his prize and let it sit on a shelf untended.
Shortly before his death, his sister happened

upon the unmarked jar in a back room and tossed
its contents out the door. Where the drops hit

the dry ground, there sprang up the wild onion,
which never withers away for good.

I am twelve. I sit by the head of my mother's bed,
watching as night falls on Lake Huron,

and we wait for the ambulance that will carry her back
to the city. The house is hushed with no one but us,

the jigsaw puzzle pieces still spread in islands,
the pines and birches going black at the open window.

The waves arrive in even rows and fold gently
on the beach. This may be when I begin

my dream of healing springs all over earth
feeding the rivers, the rains. When I begin praying

that these waters not be a myth
or a fairy tale, that they be at least as real

as the empty bedroom and the vastness
of that dark lake, its far and unseen shores.

Magic

My father liked to perform magic tricks.
At my tenth birthday party he put on a whole show

starring The Great Houdini (played by himself)
and his assistant (Don Trumble, one of his employees).

He pulled quarters out of the air, colored scarves
out of his moments-ago-empty fist, and a real rabbit

out of his black top hat. He even sawed a lady in half
(Aileen Davis, his secretary) with the saw that he used

to prune the crabapple tree and a special box
with holes for Mrs. Davis's legs to poke through.

Then he took a cake pan—empty, see?—and threw in
the quarters, a scarf, the deck of cards he'd shuffled

and cut for us, some nails, screws, pieces of string,
and his spare wand (the one that kept collapsing

when he handed it to Don). He put the lid on
the pan and began intoning a series of syllables

that seemed to go on forever before he finally
lifted the lid and bingo! There was my birthday cake!

And we ate it. Within two years he had vanished,
and I came to remember him most vividly by his

aromas: loose tobacco in his wooden cigarette box,
his cashmere sweater, and years later his fragrant

green easy chair, in which we all vied to curl up,
even though we were fully grown and just visiting

for the funeral. As if the chair were him. As if
the scarves still floated in the air above his hands.

Thank You, Edmund Waller,

for appearing on an early page of *English Literature*,
your *Go, lovely Rose* expounded by Miss Judith Phelps

in such a way that my thirteen-year-old mind
fell in love with contrasting rhymes

and syncopated three-, four-, two-, four- and four-beat lines.
Tell her that wastes her time and me

That now she knows . . . Miss Phelps was definitely *cool*,
for a girls' school, having once been spied

exiting the campus on a Friday afternoon
in a convertible, top down, driven by an actual man.

Thank you, Mr. Waller, for splicing poetry into that
fleeting scene of Judy (we called her Judy behind her back)

being sped out of the parking lot in full view.
Do I remember a scarf in the breeze? A cigarette?

(She smoked in the faculty lounge between classes.)
When I resemble her to thee / How sweet and fair

she seems to be. She loved to make us laugh,
for instance by imitating the woman in the poem

"wasting" away in "virtue," which I equated
with our chaperones, Miss Hunt and Miss Frazier,

wanting to "see daylight" between dance partners.
Miss Phelps did not return the next fall,

but your poem has returned for over forty years
(some of them seeming to lack daylight of any kind)

to go on teaching me how that heavy book can be
as light in my mind as a single page.

Buddy

On he races, "The Lost Jockey"
    of 1925, and a 1940 rerun
through a forest of table legs,
    their leaves bright with sun,

"the first canvas," Magritte said,
    "I made with the feeling I had
found my way." On he gallops
    through 1942, the year my dad

framed his print of "Man o' War,"
    fondly known as Big Red,
the champion chestnut stallion
    with the star in his forehead.

Later he showed me how to hold
    a sugar cube in my flat palm
to Buddy's velvet nose, lifted me
    into the saddle in front of him,

and taught me to curry and brush
    the nut-brown satin hide
I still lean into in my dreams.
    On through 1960 he rides,

the tip of a hoof now
    grazing the roof of a sedan
on a mountain road, with a chauffeur
    driving the bowler-hatted man.

And my life rushes on, too,
    just beginning, like Monsieur
Magritte, to find my way,
    and yet somehow never

finally: this music is silence,
    the hoofbeats all in my throat.
"Here's something for you,"
    said my father's closing note:

the liquid brown eyes
    of a chestnut thoroughbred
watching something
    just over your head.

Night Air

Trees dividing an afternoon sky
    from a lamplit street,
day and night in the same scene:
    this painting Monsieur Magritte

titled *The Empire of Lights*.
    Mysteries of the Horizon
shows three bowler-hatted men
    with a moon poised over each one.

"I detest my past," he once said
    and painted not city lights
but stars on the black houses
    under an empty sky—*Night*

and Day. Part of the past I love
    is when my father lies
on the couch on the back porch
    watching the moon rise

on a world we call "Lake Shore Drive,"
    a place of awakenings,
a dream of complete surprise
    at the eloquence of things:

the softness of cashmere,
    the smell of a cigarette,
the night air in a backyard.
    He is such a quiet man that

at times I don't understand
    what he means at all.
"Come, watch this," he whispers,
    but he may as well

shout "Wake up, we're here!"
    And for a moment there
is only one moon
    among the clouds over Lake St. Clair.

Waking on the Swiss Riviera

In the ancient temples of Aesculapius, called "hospitals,"
supplicants lay down to sleep in special oval chambers.
In the morning the priest-physician deciphered for them
the message that the gods had hidden in their dreams.

Twelve years I've lived in this southern canton,
twelve years a *straniera*, foreigner in a town
that seems far too exotic to call home.
The lake's three fountains spray thirty-foot pillars
into the radiant air, where tourists saunter
the shoreline promenade, hike the valleys,
gaze at the Titians and Raphaëls,
and sleep in a *pensione* or the Splendide
under a foot-high cloud of clean white quilt.

I arrived badly in need of an egg-shaped chamber
and lay down in the music of village accordions
under the colored lanterns of an old god.
I slept inside the boulders of this valley.
Four thousand nights I dreamed my decades
backward, undoing spells and incantations,
unwinding the stars over San Salvatore,
the crumbling shrines on her forested slopes.
I don't know if the psyche falls into chaos *in order*

to rearrange itself in a better way. I do know
that breakdown is an opening, a supplication.
Four thousand mornings I awoke and followed

the cobbled streets to work each weekday,
knowing that something else was also at work.
Time seemed at leisure in its scenic Swiss temple.
Flying, drowning, pregnant, wounded,
I carried my dream body like a sleeping child
through streets and shops, the Piazza Riforma,

paths of the Parco Civico. Slowly
my broken nights began knitting together.
I sank into the soil with the alpine snows,
bubbled in her vineyards under August sun.
I rained grief. I rained gratitude.
One afternoon, in the park behind the Kursaal,
its fountain fringed by chestnut leaves,
out of my mind at long last, I opened the eyes
within my eyes—or they opened me—

to my surprise, as if that hour were my first
real visit to earth with all its other tourists,
trams and palms and terraced hillsides,
its high meadows topped by these stony peaks
called *Dente della Vecchia,* Teeth of the Old Woman.
Twelve years now I've slept in the hospital quiet
of her nights, and it has not stopped being
exotic, this waking by day, this amazement.
It has not stopped being home.

Lattice

Inside the Villa Loreto in Paradiso a musical program
is underway, a concert of Bach played on two marimbas.

I'm alone outdoors under the portico in the evening air.
We've seen photos showing how Bach's music created

an elegant crystal lattice in each molecule of the water
that had "listened" to it. A visible polyphony.

Palm trees and cypresses line the villa's gravel driveway
along with camellia bushes, their flowers glowing white.

The wooded peaks of San Salvatore and Monte Bré
fall steeply into Lake Lugano, on which moonlight seems

to float in a carpet of shining, and we know that whatever
lives below the surface also feels that sheen flooding

its murky rooms. The night sunshine reaches even
into the cellular depths of the past lurking in the body.

Across the cobbled street, the bells of Santa Maria
degli Angioli speak to us day and night, whether we

think we hear them or not. Everything enters us,
sounds, light, wind, and tonight the healing beauty

of palms and cypresses, black mountains and silver water,
this perfectly harmonious music, strict and soft.

Copper Beech

In its tarnished silver and midnight green,
its wine-dipped leaves, and the mansions of its smoky
branches, this grand palace of a tree rising beyond your window

is Brahms's First Symphony, massive, detailed,
the opening chords surging out of silence, timpani throbbing,
the whole orchestra mounting together, then branching off

into tremolos of strings and solo voices.
As we talked through so many afternoons of your last years,
the tea- and sherry-colored dusk burnishing its dark cumulus,

the beech held up each season in its ample arms.
Once, alone, I stepped through her curtain of branches
into an inner nave, a vaulting of gray bones, gnats catching

a sliver of light, a spider descending her silk.
I stood inside her like something waiting to be born.
I remember telling you, after hearing the C Minor, that it took

Brahms fourteen years to compose it.
Longer, you said. He began listening for it long before 1862.
Is this the meaning of symphony, everyone's lives singing

together?—yours now vanished into the aromas
of your aging house, woodsmoke and rain-soaked shingles,
mine, a dangling pupa in the midday shade of her body,

my cells still infused with the pomp of that final movement
and your words about it, how much it matters whether I
bring it all down to me or allow it to lift me up.

Eagles in Chester County

The fledgling half fell, half flew
    from the raised arms of the red oak
into blue July. For forty years the wide eye
    of the reservoir had waited,

locked in the spell of sun and starlight,
    flicker and swift, with no memory
of anything like this. Generations
    of folded bones and wet down

of embryos had dried in their cracked shells,
    wind carrying no cries but ours
over the watershed and wooded shore,
    the empty crown of the white pine.

The creek runs south to the Susquehanna,
    giving up its ghosts to the clouds
as they drive back north and east.
    So the rain falls far upstream again,

and the cornfields rise as one body
    around highways and houses
leavened with dreams and incessant traffic
    between the power we once meant

to symbolize and what we pray for now:
    out of the wild plumage of night
seven thousand feathers and one heart
    fit to ride the rising thermals,

to return the land to its early seraphim,
    sunlight flaring over the rim
of the Great Valley, the shadow of healing
    spreading its wings over our sleep.

Becalmed

The aria from Zipoli's Suite in F
mirrors the glassy calm of Oxford Bay,
its pale blue milk so serene
you could walk on it from shore to shore,

its silky peace a confluence of air
and currents beneath the surface,
making these long swells
pillow the heart in a harmony so gentle

one finally considers trusting its depths.
The body knows how to weep
without any prompting
from the mind and its parade of reasons.

Tears can spring wholly formed
as if bubbled or splashed,
as if flung from vehemence or joy,
while the torso heaves, wrestling its angels,

each one an instrument with its own melody.
The violin's sadness is so keen
it hardly seems an echo from three centuries ago,
when Zipoli sang his own grief into it,

his kaddish, his requiem,
his heart's clenching and letting go.
And because he did that, someone oceans away
in time knows exactly how he felt,

feels it with a precision perfectly transcribed
onto the air of a small room.
She accepts the generous embrace
of violas, the steady measure of the bass

as calming the way hope calms,
resting spangled on water that's shattered
a distant sun into hundreds
that one can walk among in this, this, this world.

II.

The Way Home

Continental Divide

It is 1985, the summer of "Live Aid"
for relief of famine in Africa, the summer
of Rock Hudson's announcement that he's dying of AIDS.

I stand on the empty pavement of Highway 82,
12,000 feet high at the top of Independence Pass
and not much asphalt on the continent higher than this.

I'm facing east, where all the waters run
down toward the Mississippi, the Gulf Stream, the Atlantic,
east through all the landscapes of my forty-one years,

both of my parents gone into the haze
that pales the green and purple of the far summits,
the wreckage of my marriage and theirs so intertwined

I've felt I could hardly go anywhere alone.
Here between the ghost towns, emptied of their gold,
and the trickling headwaters of the Roaring Fork,

here in the summer of *Back to the Future*,
in my brand new "Live Aid" T-shirt, my white-flecked
hair doing a gusty dance, I turn around to face

into the westerly breeze, new sierras, the Pacific.
Now they are at my back, those young years.
They can read the decal: "This shirt saves lives."

I hope it does. These are gifts worth passing on:
the beckoning vista, the sudden frontier,
the rivers of days and years to come.

The Way Home

Every street here leads into mountains,
distance airbrushed layer on layer
in ever more ethereal shades of blue,

a four-part hymn in which the sopranos
are pure ether, peaks of powder-gray dust and air.
Juan Tabo, Los Rios, Happy Valley, all still

look alike to me, lined with palms,
pink oleander, and flowering prickly pear.
Can you forgive me for wanting to be happy

here, where you are not? I am preoccupied
with the daily rite of getting lost again,
while ridges rise and vanish behind tiled roofs,

and the saguaro gestures with its arms Up!
The towns are promising—El Mirage, Surprise,
wide avenues leading me southwest, then back east

and north. Fountain Hills, Thunderbird,
Superstition—just so many names right now,
but I have decided to believe in them,

even the dirt trails snaking off through succulents
into the unmapped at the heart
of each undivided block, wilderness baking

beneath these encircling heights
with their crisscrossing names: Desert Mountain,
Lone Mountain, Eagle Mountain, Paradise.

Sleeping in the Inland Sea

Tonight we wake in a Precambrian wind
that sends the mesquite leaves and acacia petals
flying like snow. Phoenix city lights waver
on the floor of the vast inland sea that is still smoothing
the rounded humps of Camelback and Squaw Peak.
Seabirds sleep in the ark of our porch,
as waves lap at the bouldered shore of Black Mountain.
The wind chimes clang like a buoy bell in the current.
We rarely speak in these 3 a.m. wakings,
preferring to reach and sleepily hold, as if words were yet
to be invented. As if we had not yet outgrown our gills.
As if the city strewn to the south like stars
were a vision, a mirage, a destination,
something our dumb clinging is meant to serve.
Where are we sailing to, packed into the hulls
of our oarless beds like so much cargo?
How many eons will it take us to reach the shore
of morning, to fit our voices around the habitual courtesies
of our old and forgetful souls?

Marking Time

She has been buying clocks from the catalogs
tossed on the dining table in a sea of sweepstakes

and charities: wall clocks, mantel clocks, miniature
grandfather clocks, a pair of plastic ornamental chimers

with three battery doors in the back (two for $18)
all over the house, plus nine broken watches:

all her eighty-nine years ticking, humming, pulsing
silently, saying nothing. "Mother, we don't need

another kitchen clock!" "We do too! I can't see the clock
on the stove when I'm standing here at the sink!"

Her mind is a shopful of cuckoos and alarms,
but what is the meaning of "tomorrow" if not this

tension, this energy stored in the coiled spring?
Her future dwindles, yet looms larger every day.

No wonder she halts the minutes with their names.
What does it matter if she can't tell 8:00 from 20 to 12?

Or if a.m. and p.m. trade places? Some nights
we wake to her glimmering like a ghost in our bedroom,

fully dressed, wrapped in her trench coat, ready to go
home, a destination no longer on this earth for her.

"Mother, let's you and me take a little walk." She gets lost
roaming the three-bedroom maze of our house.

Back in bed, she slips as quickly as Einstein's thought
through the landscape of time, till our talk slows,

and she dozes again, and the second hand sweeps up
the stillness. Dust settles grain by grain on the bedside

table, and on her glasses, each lens an hourglass
with its little hill of sand. As glowing hour hands sink

imperceptibly, a digital pulse counts out
the last remnants of dark, the approach of dawn.

Furnace

The house is so quiet I can hear the earth's
molten core rumbling up through the furnace.

I've lain down on the couch to listen,
and I lie very still, just as I imagine her

lying in this last afternoon of her body,
ninety years old and finally a bride of fire,

no more bothered by flames now
than by the barrage of neutrinos diving angelic

through bone and stone. Whatever fire is.
Sun-feathers caught in earth's rough coat.

How many times did she make us promise
their quick mercy? Today she enters anew

the mystery of Heraclitus' *ever-living fire*,
of which all things are made, the portal

to what we still think of as nothing.
A few pounds of ash. My body warms

on its sunward side. Each of my hairs leaps
with brightness in the 93-million-mile-wide

halo looking for things to light on.
And my heart makes such a soft drumming

I can barely hear it above the roar
of heartbeats of all the living and all the dead

who surround and warm and touch us
so tenderly we don't notice it at all.

Phoenix

In the citywide heat sink of asphalt and tile,
she burns all day overhead, white with intensity,

soaring so low that the fire of her wings
boils our cell juices in their delicate jackets.

When the temperature at the intersection of Bell
and El Mirage reaches 120, and the car is a kiln,

when back at home, I gaze out the hot front window
into an empty street that could fry our dinner,

when a malignancy first awakens the once quiet
night of my X-ray film, and I see it clearly in

black and white on the screen, the 2 a.m. ceiling,
the inside of my eyelids, I finally hear in the hush

of my own dark a question: *Now, girl,*
which myth will you choose to live inside?

Sizzling highways coil at the interchange
in a low brown cloud of smog, a vague, perpetual

dust storm enveloping all to the south,
while over our street, the wide sky offers another

story, its cloudless blue, and later its fierce firebird.
I have seen her red and gold feathers

in the west at dusk and known she is busy again
lining her nest with spices: night breeze, mesquite,

crushed creosote leaves. Then the creaking daily
machinery of starting over. "Do I have

the strength for this?" I ask. *Give it all you've got,*
she sings, *and you will be given just enough more.*

Bright Angel Point

Gazing into the Grand Canyon's vast sunken garden
    of peaks, its walls glowing coppery rose,

the handiwork of millions of years, I hold onto the iron
    railing with both hands. The air is so steeped

in rust and sunlight, its currents so sweeping
    and keen, you could easily sail right off the edge

of this promontory a mile above Bright Angel Creek,
    its quicksilver spilling into the Colorado's

flowing signature to this empire of stone. Two weeks old
    in my new body, I'm a fabulous creature, half-

woman, half-tomboy, with no visible stitching, just a river
    of dry blood threading the plain of my right ribs,

my new shape having been carved out in just over an hour,
    so soft is flesh in the path of the scalpel.

Suddenly I envy this slow erosion, the leisure of water
    at work separating the yielding from the firm,

wearing away one foot of Coconino sandstone every
    million years, leaving these slopes awash

in sunrise and dotted with only those trees able to
    keep a grip. This journey brings me to the brink

of thin air, to a buoyancy I've never felt before, a suspicion
    of canyons everywhere underfoot, just waiting

for some trickle to persist, finally, in removing grain by grain
    the ground we stand on, while over the same eons

the hardest stone grows taller amid losses, until,
    like this sweetly named point, it holds us briefly

at a peak: earth as a candle, I as a flame, willful,
    eating the wind of the future, and hungry for more.

Lunch Hour

A suntanned jogger with blond ponytail
bobs through the dappled aisle of willows
and cottonwoods on the lakeside path. Bicyclists

glide by a granny with cane and companion
and a toddler hurling handfuls of breadcrumbs
at congregations of ducks, coots, and Canada geese.

I'm already dropping crumbs from my sandwich
by the time I settle onto a wrought-iron bench
and lean back on its warm brass plaque:

"In Memory of Kathleen Mooney. 1998."
In my purse the folded message about Alexandra,
diagnosed in the same year as I was and now

gone. Her blondish brush-cut in middle age,
her tomboy slightness, and soft voice all deceptive
—"I'm *driven* to finish my novel, *Yin Fire!*"—

and she did. The charcoal-feathered coots
have arrived on the grass nearby, sleek and homely,
their blood-red eyes wary, white beaks slanting

from their black foreheads, Egyptian, priestly,
emissaries from another realm, patient, grazing as if
disinterested. One waddles up close to my bench,

settles down in a puddle of its own plumage,
and eventually half-sleeps. I chew my sandwich
and let the sun burn through my sweater,

heating my hair, baking my bones in their slips
of muscle and fat, till I half-sleep, too,
seeing through slit eyes the willow veil

and the palms beyond, and beyond that
South Mountain hoisting the blue on its back,
as if holding the ethereal back from this noon path

with its sateen water, its bicycle bells, its flocks
of wings rising, and all our Kathleens, in this
hour of appetite, this brief waking sleep.

Soft Touch

We've watched the wild pigs at the water pot
rubbing muzzle to rump, their bristly itching

and grooming, the lioness stretching out in the shade
on the zoo's Africa Trail, cooling her creamy belly.

I shower before bed and cool my limbs on the sheets
and read that puppies deprived of their mother's

licking stop growing. Even injections of growth
hormones don't induce them to grow.

The lioness scratched her back against packed dirt.
The kittens encamping on Mother's home hospital bed

allowed us to brush our noses into their underhairs.
Two wild piglets pushed through their mother's forelegs

and hindlegs to yank at her teats. Eyes closed,
my promiscuous nerves can sometimes fail to distinguish

Peter's sleepy touch from Arthur's paid and trained
massage, and both men must compete with hypnotic

subtleties of pillow and breeze. So yes, it was also a gift
to be weaned early into the world's tenderness:

water's silks, wind's brush, the bristling
excitement of pushing in to suck at the sweet milk.

Heart's Mountains

In 1777, Goethe put his boot in the stirrup
and rode alone into the foothills of the Brocken.

I drive Highway 87 north from the desert floor
past Four Peaks into the White Mountains.

I had not learned any German when I first
heard his poem title mentioned (in church choir),

"Harzreise im Winter," and I thought "Really?
Hearts rise in winter?" I took it as true, somehow,

and the music Brahms made of it was so moving,
I knew it was praying for all of us. Goethe

felt that being outdoors with natural ground
under our feet allows *strength and power*

to run into us from the soil like sap.
In a time of discouragement he rode for weeks

through the rugged Harz country, its sunlit mists
cloaking him with light. Brahms felt the same

power rising when he set that journey's verse
as a rhapsody for his own heart's comfort.

At the edge of the Rim Trail, the earth drops
steeply, then resumes its sea of evergreen

slopes and summits, today dusted with snow,
distance, and stillness outside of time.

I never open my journal on trail walks,
and yet I can never bear to leave it behind.

Then once I'm home, out pours the ponderosa-
scented air, smell of the saddle and horse,

earth underfoot, and the rhapsody's voices
filling one room of the winter night.

Lamplight

In your favorite chair, under the Tiffany dragonfly lamp,
you sit rereading *Lost Splendour,* taking yourself back
through the 1890s to the beautiful Princess Yusúpova,
the richest woman in all Imperial Russia, her diamonds
rainbowed in firelight as she dines with her two young sons.

Our grandfather clock ticks steadily on. The radio
pours a nocturne over us, while under the dragonflies'
ruby eyes and their amber and black-veined wings,
the high ceilings and satin-lined halls of Archangel Palace
echo with voices. You are a ghost of the future visiting

a past that haunts our house. I've read this book too,
her diamonds prisming fire, the blue damask walls,
and the rock crystal chandelier, so I'm a ghost beside you
at the dinner in her sitting room, the whole vast palace
present in the cone of lamplight pooling in your lap.

Ours is a reproduction, of course. Tiffany stained his
original flares just as the Princess's orchestra playing
"Paradis du Rêve" and her dining room set for hundreds
with gold plates and candles were sliding with the Empire
into war, revolution, exile, remnants, charity. But tonight

those massive tragedies sleep in the unread pages.
The century has not yet turned, both her sons are alive,
her jewels still sparkle, and you and I are thousands of miles
and over a hundred years away, holding their story,
as we are held, wingtip to wingtip in a circle of light.

Picturing Love

"When I make a photograph, I make love,"
said Stieglitz in 1918, the year
of the worldwide epidemic and the year

he installed O'Keeffe in his niece's top-floor
studio to recover from influenza.
Sun through the tall windows and skylight

bounced off pale yellow walls in all directions.
Slowly, inside this cocoon, she started
to paint again. In the hot, sunlit room

they became lovers. And he began
to photograph her: her open hand pressed
to her naked breasts, her pale face and black hair

framed by the giant painted seeds
and swirls of her canvas. He worked, she said,
"with a kind of heat and excitement,"

with a certain elemental chemistry,
her body ghosting itself onto his glass plates
coated with grains of photosensitive silver halides. Light

coming in the open lens makes these grains unstable
and ready to darken . . . . My husband tinkers
for hours with these reactions,

the tungsten photofloods heating and cooling.
In the arboretum he focuses on flowers,
hauling them in huge through the small aperture,

tidal waves of petals, the precise landscape
of the plump dusted ovaries,
their geography of flaws developing perfectly.

The photoelectric storm blows even at night:
even moonlight wakens the delicate silver.
Night and day our bodies stream out in all

directions, transmitting light, energy, intent,
continuing to touch across the varying
spaces between us. Subtle as fragrance,

even his absence can seed my solitude,
the faintest starlight falling on my sheets
swelling buds, articulating folds.

Moonbath: A Lullaby

Tonight the moon is a perfect pearl,
a seed floating in each eye as you gaze
up into earth's softest sunbath,
photons fresh in from a lunar landing,

but weary of miles, ninety-three million out
to the iron-rich seas and glassy meadows
of a four-billion-year-old crater-pocked rock
and back to earth. Are you sleepy yet?

Tonight the moon is a snowfall,
light as particles drifting over your face,
your eyelids heavy, fine muscles letting go.
Can you feel the motes sifting down

through the stratosphere's filmy clouds
to land easy on your inner arms?
Tonight's moon is a tarnished mirror,
a high whole note the coyotes call to,

their blind instinctual throat-ache unspooling.
It's a waterfall tired of its rainbows,
turning everything earthly to smoke
and ashes, the day's flock of angels

finding your body celestial enough to rest on.
Can you feel them alighting on long hairs
and fine ones like mist on grasses?
Breathe in, and each cell drinks

its drop of moondew, white fire gently
warming and cooling exactly as prayed for.
Tonight the moon is a birch leaf
caught in the solar wind streaming past us

toward Pluto, undiminished,
like the hymn welling up in your limbs
at last to nearly audible, as you sail out
into deep space now, singing with sleep.

Andromeda Galaxy

How did they manage to sleep, the Greeks,
  with all those shrieks and groans reeling overhead?
We can hardly even recall why the poor girl
  was chained to a cliff ledge or how Perseus flying by
on his winged sandals happened to land exactly

on her shore. What's over our heads tonight is M31,
  the great spiral galaxy we think of as the twin
of our own Milky Way. The daughter was being punished
  by the gods, ever inexact in justice, for her mother's
vanity, and there is the Queen Cassiopoeia herself,

a five-star W, with her husband King Cepheus,
  and Perseus holding aloft the head of the Gorgon
Medusa, an eclipsing binary star that we still know
  by its Arabic name of *Algol*, meaning *ghoul*.
So were these just stories, fictions the ancients made up

out of whole cloth? Andromeda's galaxy is No. 31
  in Philippe Messier's eighteenth-century catalog
of one hundred "fuzzy-looking objects" in the heavens.
  Counting was his myth. In 2002 Robert Gendler
made a digital mosaic of 20 frames photographed

through a small telescope (our version of winged sandals),
  capturing light that had traveled for two million
years to stain his page with a gossamer oval of pale
  bluish-white. Is that what we look like in our whirling
splash of milk? Is she our mirror? The Greeks might

well ask how we manage to sleep so alone in the vast
   night with all these numbers, without the company
of tales woven around a kernel as mysterious
   as the origin of Andromeda's double nucleus
and the amniotic (my myth) smudge of our own.

In the Light Before Sunrise,

in bed with the sheets thrown back, I'm reading
The Hours, your copy, loaned for the summer.
In this novel, Clarissa is preparing to give
a party in New York, just as Mrs. Dalloway
did in Woolf's novel, and as you are

doing today in Boston, buying flowers
and fabrics in lilac and green for your son's
engagement. I come to page ninety-seven,
whose corner you've folded down—to mark
your place, I thought, but now I think

maybe not. I, too, stop at *How often since then*
has she wondered what might have happened if . . . ?
I imagine you pausing here to watch what
other lives might have been yours.
Clarissa sees it is possible that her life

could have been different. As if inside
each party, a *might have been* party's in progress,
with its own décor and dessert buffet, say,
in yellow roses and white orchids, a party
for your *might have been* daughter. Or mine.

I even imagine my own life dramatized,
novelized, by the richness of one huge regret—
my very own Peter Walsh back from India,
"*the* might have been," as Lowell put it
to Bishop. Or at least by the company

of multiple *if only*'s lurking in the wings,
unlived, unmarred, unforgotten,
lending the sense that this life was chosen
(or fated from within, which comes to
the same thing), that it's mine

out of more than happenstance, this summer
morning in bed with a book and its *what if*'s,
while in through the screen waft all the days
that I won't ever experience wrapped
like spice inside the one that I will.

Reading Chopin

In her one hundredth year, her memory holds
the century like sunlight with all its motes in motion.
With the last faint glow of her eyesight gone,
I read to her from *Chopin, His Life and Works,* her choice,
and already the notes have begun to cascade down
the insides of our minds, shimmering, liquid.
Curled up on her couch, I read into her good right ear,
and we try to picture Liszt, Mendelssohn, Berlioz,
and Chopin all gathered in one Parisian salon,
the young Pole at the keyboard and all whispers hushed.
She leans toward me till our heads almost
touch. "Margaret," she says in an accent mingling pre-1933
German, Haifa Hebrew, and half a century of Phoenix.
"I feel as if I can still hear Rubinstein playing
in Berlin. The whole concert hall was mesmerized.
It must have been in the '20s"—years before
she joined the wave of emigrées, refugees
lugging their bundles, their hidden treasures as secretly
as Chopin had carried abroad with him
tunes of the Polish countryside, as migrations everywhere
cart their baggage along with the weightless, precious
myrrh of knowledge. In the inch of air
between her lightly peppered white hair and mine,
Parisian candlelight blooms,
Germany listens, and whole tribes move across
the Asian plain under moonlight
to the music of what the book calls *his insight
into the secret places of the heart.* "Yes!" she whispers.

And it is all here now, loosely bound in her wrinkled skin:
night music, heartbreaking passages, oceans
of time, and the islands on which we sometimes meet.

Night Blooming in Paul Klee

Having spent all day as a draftee
slathering gray paint on bomber wings and bodies,
while planes flew and crashed around him
in the loud Bavarian air,

he returned at dusk to his quiet room, where,
from muddy fields and the waste of war,
he drew a vivid hue, a twilight and midnight blue
through his brush into *Night*

Flowers, 1918: uncurling ferns and palm
fronds, a rocket-shaped watchtower, a pendant
sunflower, and a black orb all swim in a sea
of sapphire and ultramarine.

With so many fellow painters dead—August Macke
fallen at Perthes, Franz Marc in the mud
of Verdun—Klee was exempted
from front-line duty and so did his best,

while the planes roared overhead, to dive through
iris and blackberry blue to a beauty
one note deeper than dread. *This week,* he wrote,
we had three fatal casualties; one man

was smashed by the propeller, the other two crashed
from the air. Yesterday, a fourth came plowing into the roof

of the workshop, turned a somersault, and collapsed
upside down in a heap of wreckage.

I drive the Pima Freeway home with war news
on the radio and the sky stained with smoky liquid,
a purple and tulip-red cloud smear,
a blue-bottle aura, tinctures of air

as untouchable as music. The work day's end
is the dawn of another kind of mind, half-enchanted,
as lush as carpets of roadside lupine
as rich and pure as his palette.

The car radio relays the sounds of gunfire
from time zone to time zone, reporting on dawn
flushing the desert air over there
while here, to the west of the freeway,

the last of our dusky pink is being charcoaled out.
To the sound of bombers heading
home empty, I'm all too glad to drive on
into the magical blues

of his painting, *Nächtliche Blumen,*
which I like to translate as "Night Flowers,"
because it does. Remember this morning's live update
from the hotel? *Night is falling on Baghdad,*

and we can see the explosions. We see them, too,
the sudden white blooms, even though evening rises
like a blue morning glory closing around us,
or a bushful of larkspur,

that bouquet held in the ground's fist,
its very slow explosions of indigo opening
into violet-white at the heart of each floweret,
the wild eyes of the world.

Angel's Landing

Something celestial about these buttes,
maroon-pink rock rising half a mile heavenward,

drives the mind to devotional naming:
Three Patriarchs, the explorers called them,

Great White Throne, Altar of Sacrifice, Zion.
Earth's aging is laid bare here in layer on layer

of vertical desert suspended in stillness,
the silence of dinosaur-age stone in the blown

and shifting dunes they wandered, sculpted
by the Virgin River's sudden grinding torrents.

Walking the trail upstream and down today
between the invisible mouth and delta,

I think of my friend in her one hundredth year
blind but seeing clearly in her mind's eye,

and of my new niece in the very first days
of her life, emerging from her embryonic sleep,

and of the billions of us in between them.
I think that something from my friend is

already on its way to this baby. I don't know
how. Herta to me to Annie to Rachel and Ben

and into the tiny perfect ear they nuzzle. But not
just via me. Something that began a century ago

and even before that in central Europe has
migrated—Frankfurt, Tel Aviv, Phoenix—and joined

the diaspora that the child is surrounded by
as surely as we are now by these cliffs watching

parentally over their valley. Does anyone doubt
these legacies? That what generations ago

was sown into the wind, some words or gestures
and their now distant ripples, has been borne

over tundra, Pacific, Sierra Nevada on westerly
currents, cleansed of words? Our winter pilgrimage

pauses in this magical place, where gifts arrive
like sunlight—one cannot look into their

source directly, only receive their warmth
through closed eyes and feel renewed. What we

thought was hard and fast splits and lets go,
relaxes into the landslide's half-suspended falling.

A cliff in all its adamant calm goes to pieces,
becomes a shawl, a waterfall of rubble

and sand. So we soften and find new ground.
Clear river water, liquid amber and jade,

talks its bubbling talk and carries away
its modest daily tonnage, awaiting the chance

to tear a few more centuries down
from these heights, this Angel's Landing,

this touching of whole and broken worlds
dressed all day in the colors of dawn.

Rereading *Four Quartets*

When the year 1962 was inscribed in this book,
one of your last Christmas gifts, I was eighteen,
your eldest. What did I understand of these quartets?

Or of all that had happened, and would happen, to you?
You were gone before I knew what I would be
thanking you for in different forms all these years.

I've read them in several dorm rooms, mine
and others', seduced by their music and high calling,
but not understanding much, still being a Prufrock,

enamored with walking the same Cambridge streets
Eliot had walked, feeling his book's strange weight
in my hands when he died in my junior year.

In my rooms on Via Roncaccio with the view
through palms and cypresses to Lugano's roofs
and slopes falling steeply into the lake, with the lights

of Corona twinkling at the summit of San Salvatore,
I read them. Among cobbled streets and piazzas,
I learned more about the waste land than I wanted to.

I read them in a two-room apartment in Pennsylvania,
its tall windows filled with oak and maple leaves
filtering the fluorescent aura of science labs

and the globes of street lamps glowing on collegiate
gothic façades and lit night windows, when all I did
was annotate, comprehending even less.

Last night I read them with the lights of Phoenix
wavering in the dusk beyond palms, mesquite,
and one tall cypress taper beside Black Mountain.

And today I read them on my lunch hour at work.
I've always pictured Burnt Norton as a charred ruin,
and now I learn that this manor house was named

for the former house that had burned down.
Burnt Norton, with its rose garden, rose from ashes,
haunted but whole. *Home is where one starts from,*

he says. Actually I am coming to feel that home
is what I travel toward, search for, learn to find,
and that this dialogue is part of the destination.

Traffic streams north and south on Hayden,
as I close up the office at five into rooms full
of a medley of grays and sun through slatted blinds.

I let the CD play on through Track 3:
"Transformation" for flute, cello, and strings.
Cars move, music moves, even the light moves,

but I don't move for a minute, while something
passes through me, *a lifetime burning in every moment.*
I've asked myself what I want to live to a hundred

for. Now I try out an answer: to understand
these lines, these movements, this music you
have given me, a life that goes on unfolding

as if it meant to gradually gloss every image
and phrase in this poem I have barely begun to
fathom, and for which I thank you again:

the endless task, the workday ending in revelation,
a moment of presence infused with past,
future, poetry, sunlight, music, and mystery.

Notes

"Sleeping with Nietzsche." Sils Maria is the village in the Swiss Engadine where Nietzsche spent several summers in the 1880s and where he wrote portions of *Thus Spake Zarathustra*. "Humans might . . ." This voice is imagined, not quoted.

"Gibbous Moon." Newton is quoted in Diana Breuton's *Many Moons* (New York: Prentice Hall Press, 1991), p. 218.

"For Sale." Spinoza's *Ethics*, Third Part, Proposition LIX, "The Affects, Definition XIII, Explanation" in *Spinoza Selections*, John Wild, ed. (New York: Charles Scribner's Sons, 1930), p. 270. Lao Tsu, *Tao Te Ching*, lines from No. 22, my composite version.

"Buddy." "the first canvas . . ." Remark by René Magritte reported by E.C. Goossen, quoted in Harry Torczyner, *Magritte, Ideas and Images*, trans. Richard Miller (New York: Harry N. Abrams Inc., 1977), p. 48.

"Night Air." "I detest . . ." Suzi Gablik, *Magritte* (Thames and Hudson, 1988), p. 17.

"Waking on the Swiss Riviera." The epigraph is composed from information from Fred Alan Wolf's *The Dreaming Universe* (New York: Simon & Schuster, 1994), pp. 67–68, and various other sources.

"Lattice." Photographs of water crystals by Masaru Emoto, *The True Power of Water*, trans. Noriko Hosoyamada (Beyond Words Publishing, 2005), p. 155.

"Heart's Mountains." "Strength and power . . ." This is Goethe rendered by Thomas Mann, *Lotte in Weimar* (Berkeley: University of California Press, 1968), p. 340. Brahms used verses from *"Harzreise im Winter"* as the text for his "Alto Rhapsody."

"Lamplight." Prince Felix Youssoupoff, *Lost Splendor* (New York: G.P. Putnam's Sons, 1953), p. 62 and passim.

"Picturing Love." "When I make . . ." Stieglitz is quoted in
Roxanna Robinson's *Georgia O'Keeffe, A Life* (New York:
Harper & Row, 1989), p. 251.

"Andromeda Galaxy." "Fuzzy-looking objects" is from
Ian Ridpath and Wil Tirion, *The Monthly Sky Guide*,
fourth edition (Cambridge University Press, 1996),
p. 11. Robert Gendler's photograph is available at
http://antwrp.gsfc.nasa.gov/apod/ap021021.html.

"In the Light Before Sunrise,." "How often since then . . ."
Michael Cunningham, *The Hours* (New York: Picador USA,
2002), p. 97. "*the* might have been," Robert Lowell and
Saskia Hamilton (ed.), *The Letters of Robert Lowell* (New
York: Farrar Straus and Giroux, 2005) p. 289, letter to
Elizabeth Bishop of August 15, 1957.

"Reading Chopin." "His insight . . ." *Encyclopedia Britannica*,
2002 edition, Volume 3, p. 264.

"Night Blooming in Paul Klee." "This week . . ." *The Diaries of
Paul Klee, 1898-1918,* edited by Felix Klee (Berkeley:
University of California Press, 1968), entry 1106, 2.21,
February 21, 1918, p. 387. "Night is falling . . ." Anne Garrels,
Foreign Correspondent for NPR, reporting from Baghdad,
April 2003.

"Rereading *Four Quartets*." "Home is where . . ." and "a lifetime
burning . . ." T. S. Eliot, *Four Quartets*, "East Coker," part V,
lines 19 and 23 in *Collected Poems, 1909-1950* (New York:
Harcourt Brace & World, Inc., 1962), p. 129.